To Samantha,
With love always
Mom-Mom

Congratulations

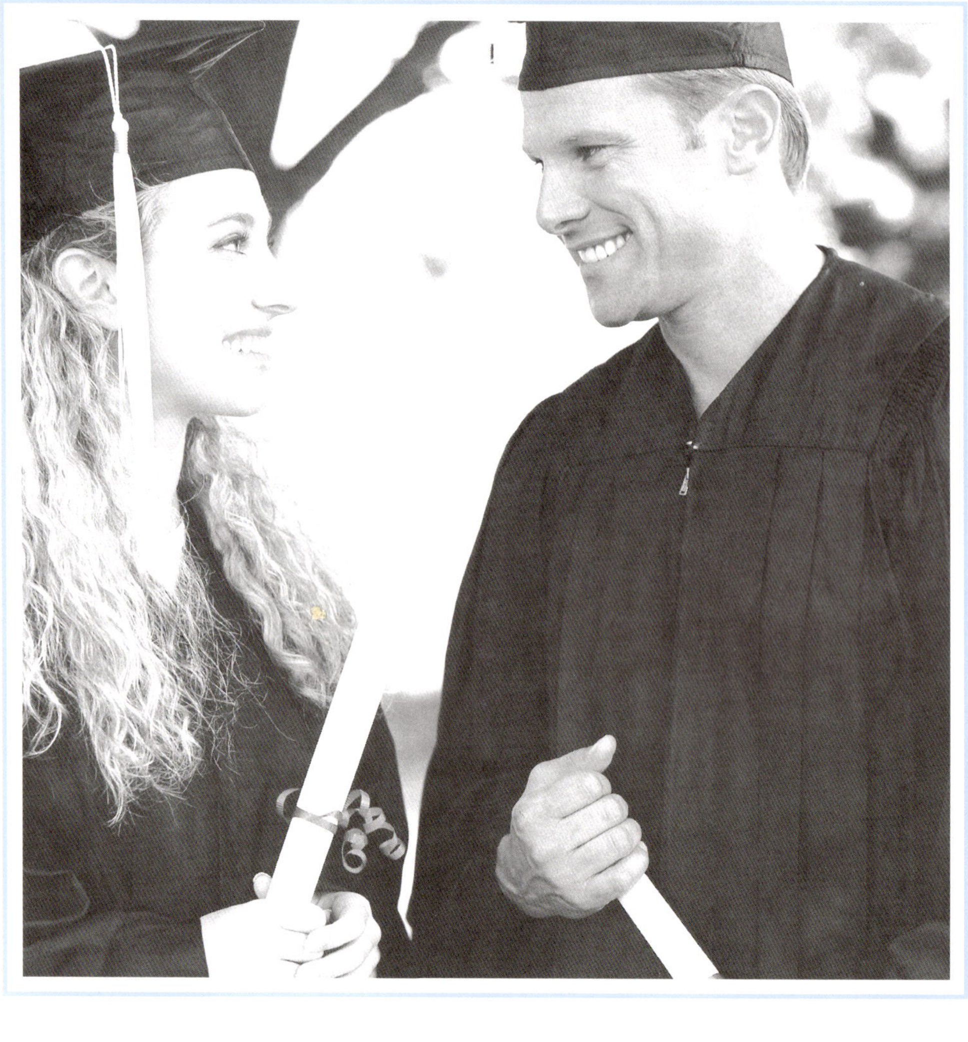

*Hail to you,
graduate,
your future awaits!*

I will raise my glass

The greatest of these have been

All the academics, of course, but much more important and impressive to me was always being true to yourself and "staying the course", especially when that meant not being included in some things by some "friends". You've discovered truth conquers all.

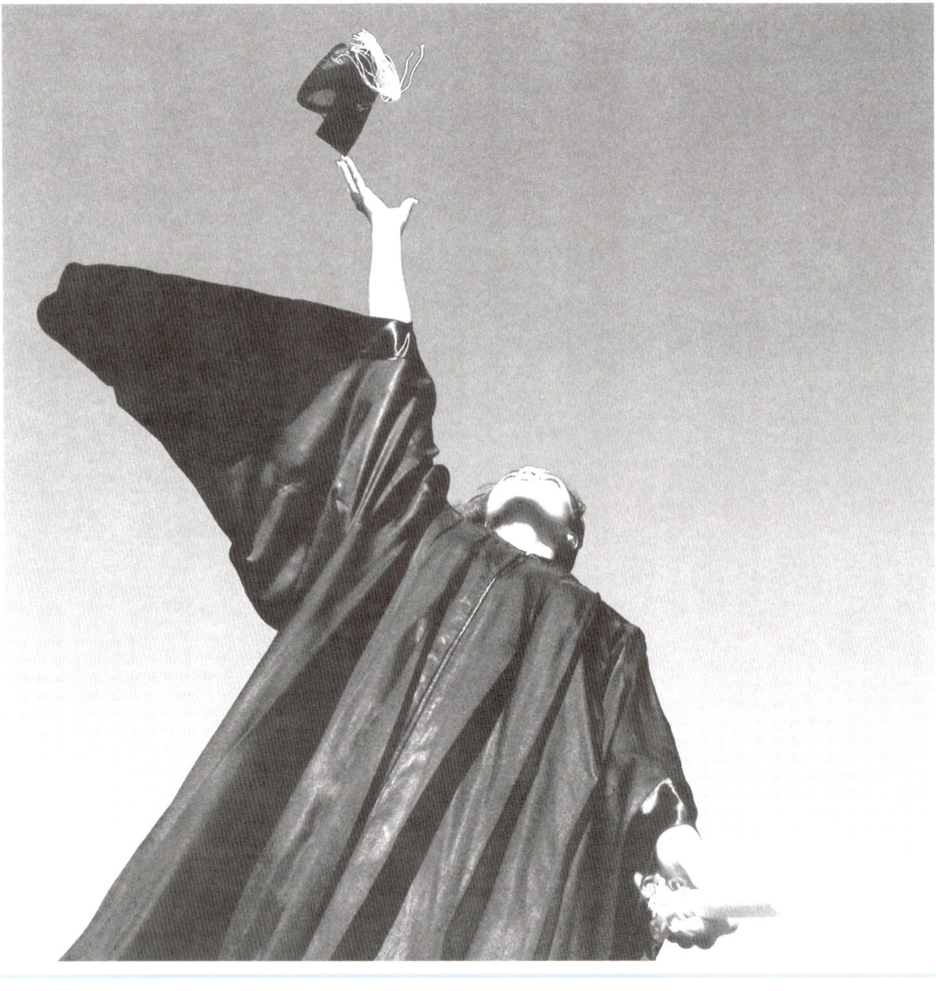

*You've worked so hard
and now you have made it!
Congratulations
Graduate!*

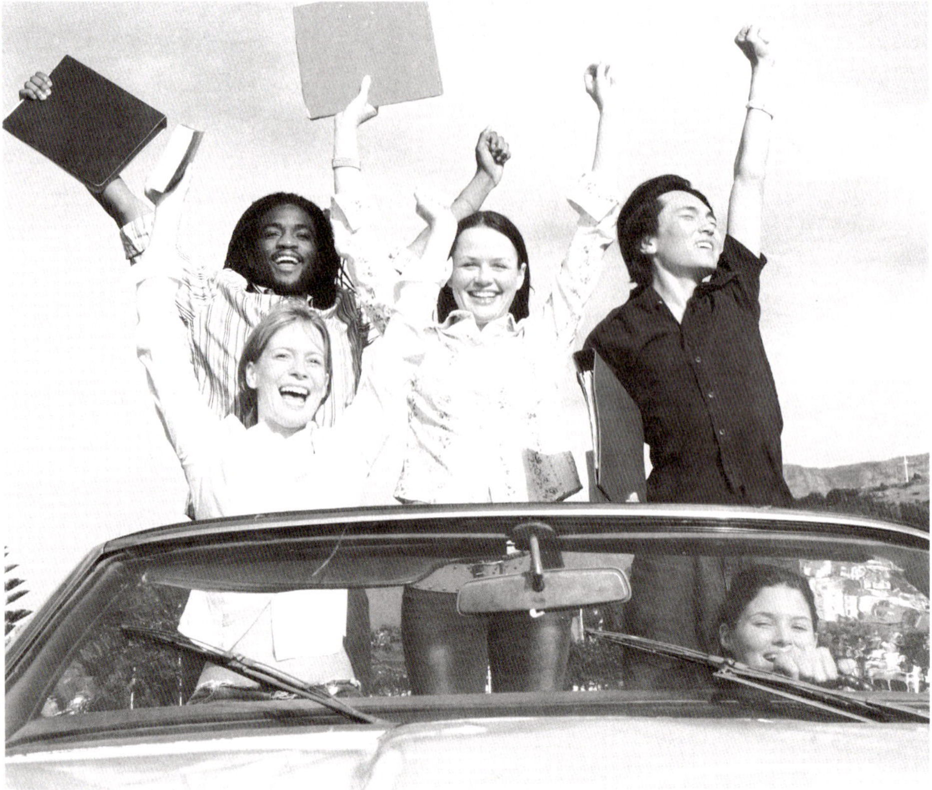

This is the memory I hold close to me

It matters most to me that you are always fair, kind and considerate, but I'll always treasure the first time Pop and I took you out to dinner — Mickey D's — and you ate three orders of french fries. You were only eight months old.
How about being afraid of E.T., or the foxes that lived in the woods behind my house, or thunderstorms at the mountain house? I could fill a book.

I recommend you for finishing

You were relieved to finish

I dont remember you ever being a quitter, but I know you were happy when school was over each year. You were happy when you were finally finished with braces and piano lessons, too.

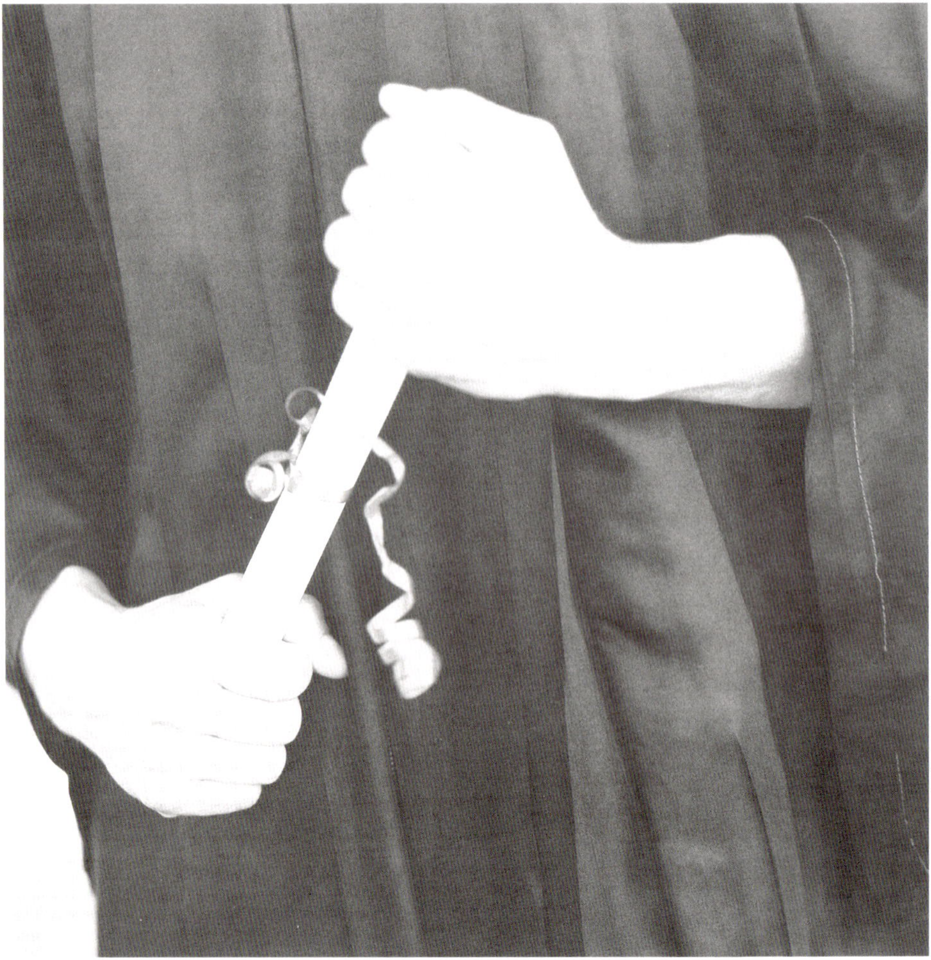

Recognize yourself as an accomplished graduate!

I love the

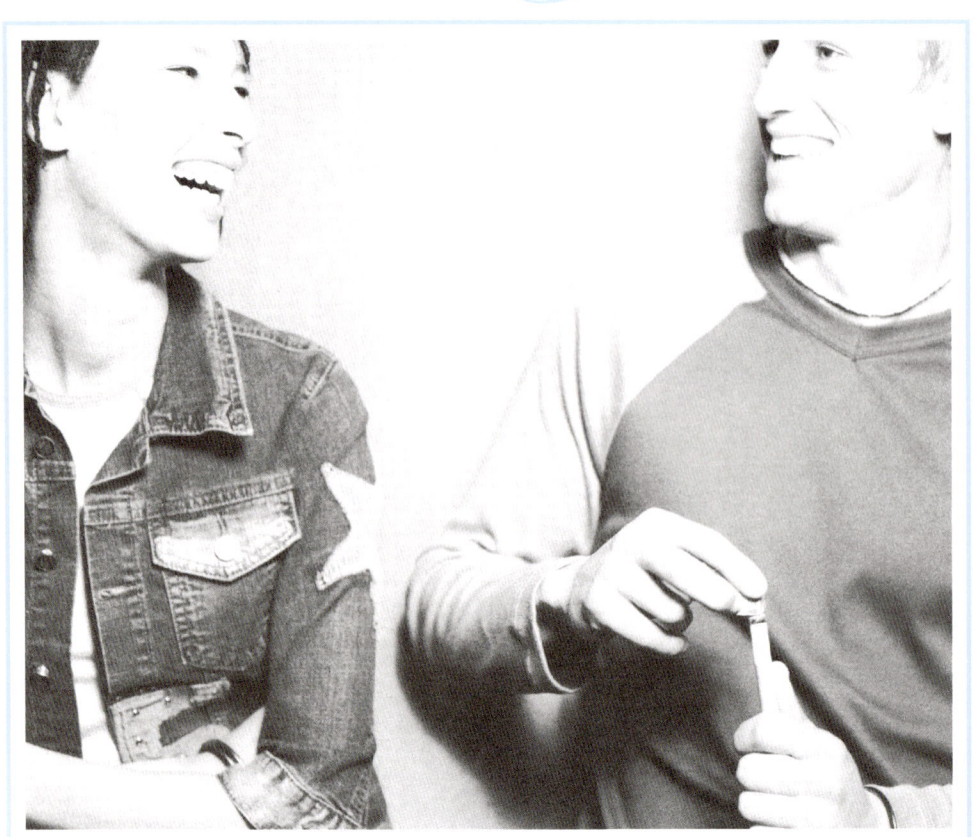

sound of your laughter.

This is when I've heard it the most

Just all the fun we have whenever we're together, but especially when we pulled up next to those guys at the redlight with our tuxes cranked in W.B.G. What about "migrant religious workers" or Pop trying to get us to say "bell" during charades at mountain house Christmas?

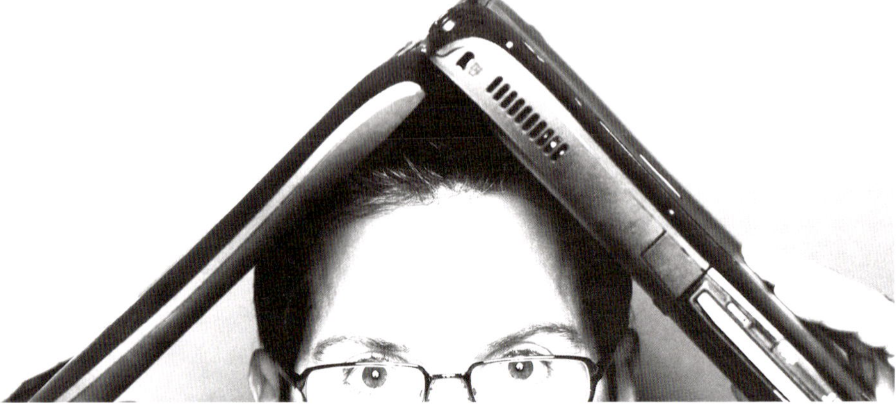

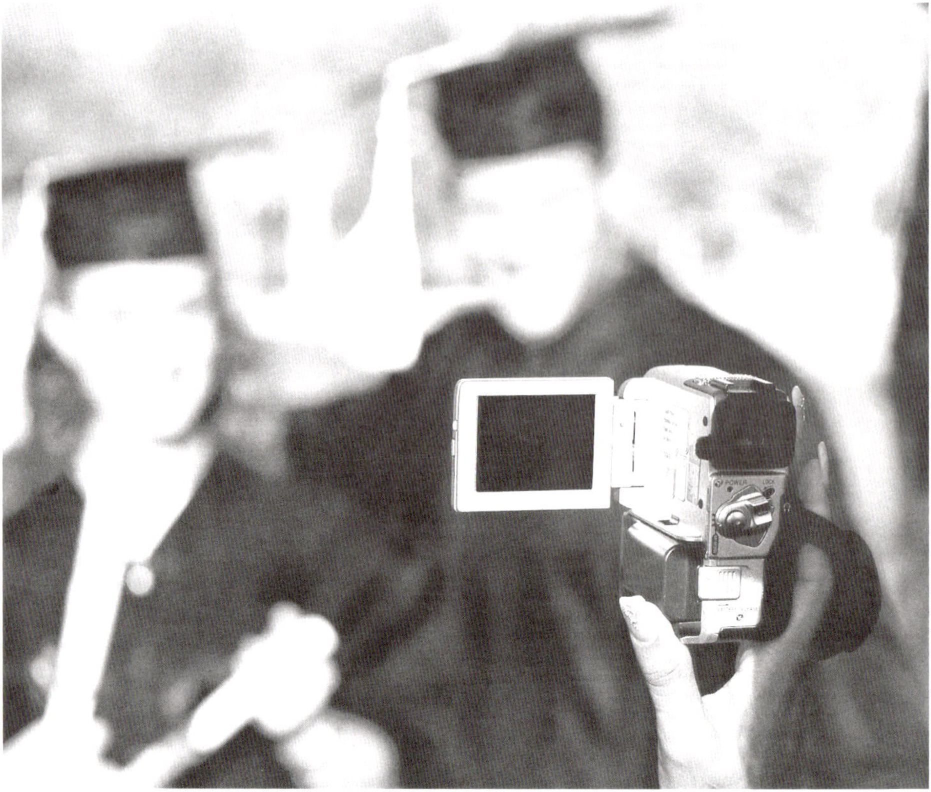
POWER
LOCK

Your family is proud of the person you have become

Because you are your own person and won't compromise your integrity. Any rewards you'll get will be because you had a plan, worked hard and never gave up.

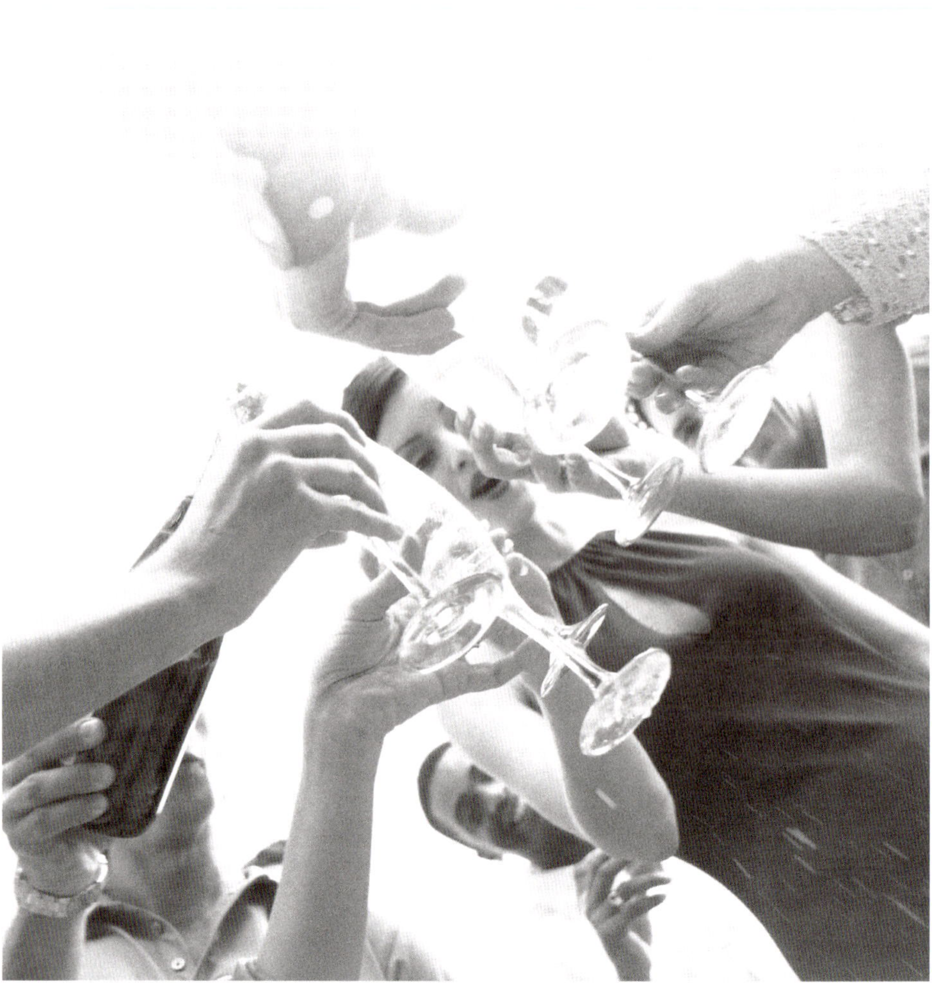

Congratulations!

I'll bet your next step is going to be to complete your education, but hopefully a lot of personal growth, challenging and testing life and a ton of fun. Don't be afraid to take a risk sometimes.

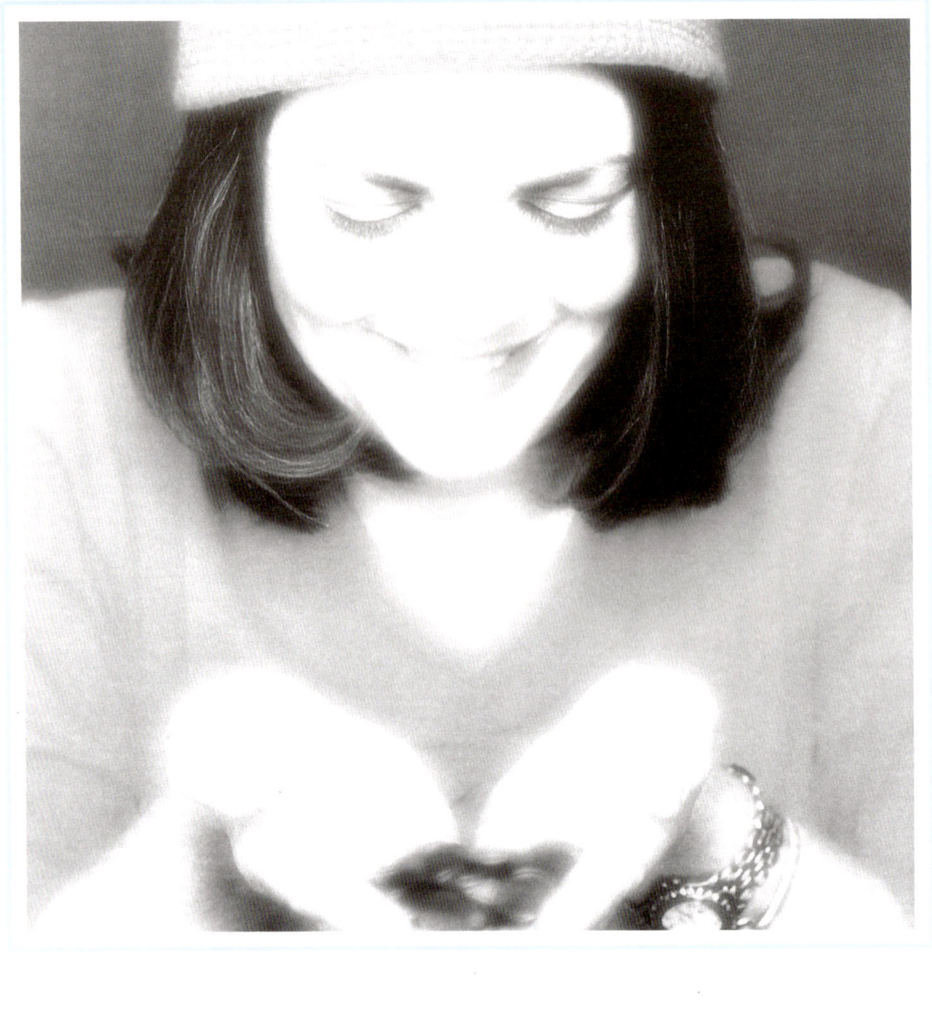

*Wishing
you a future full
of happiness*

You have

...much praise for others.

A mentor you learned much from

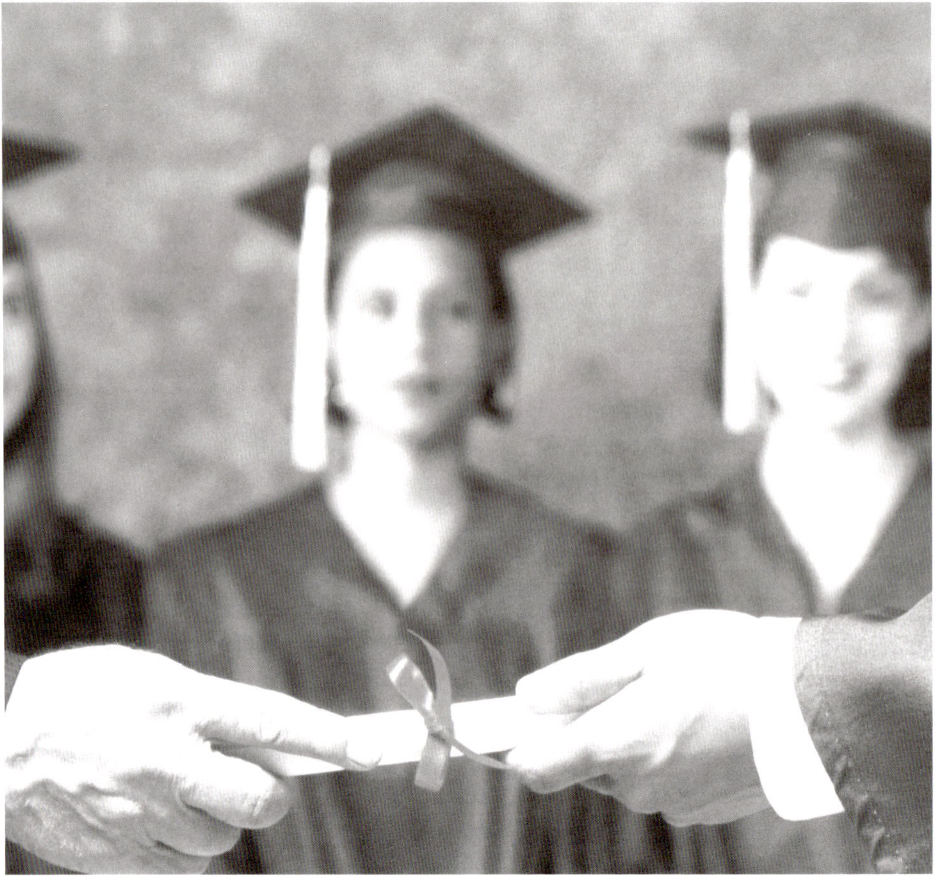

*You have a world
to look forward to.
What will you make of it?*

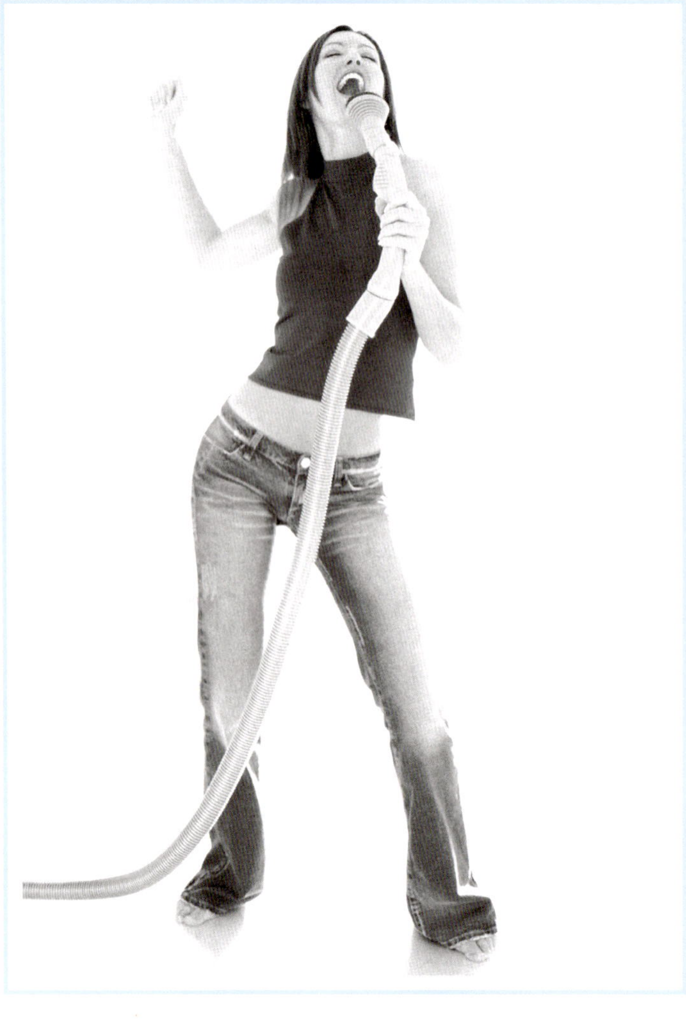

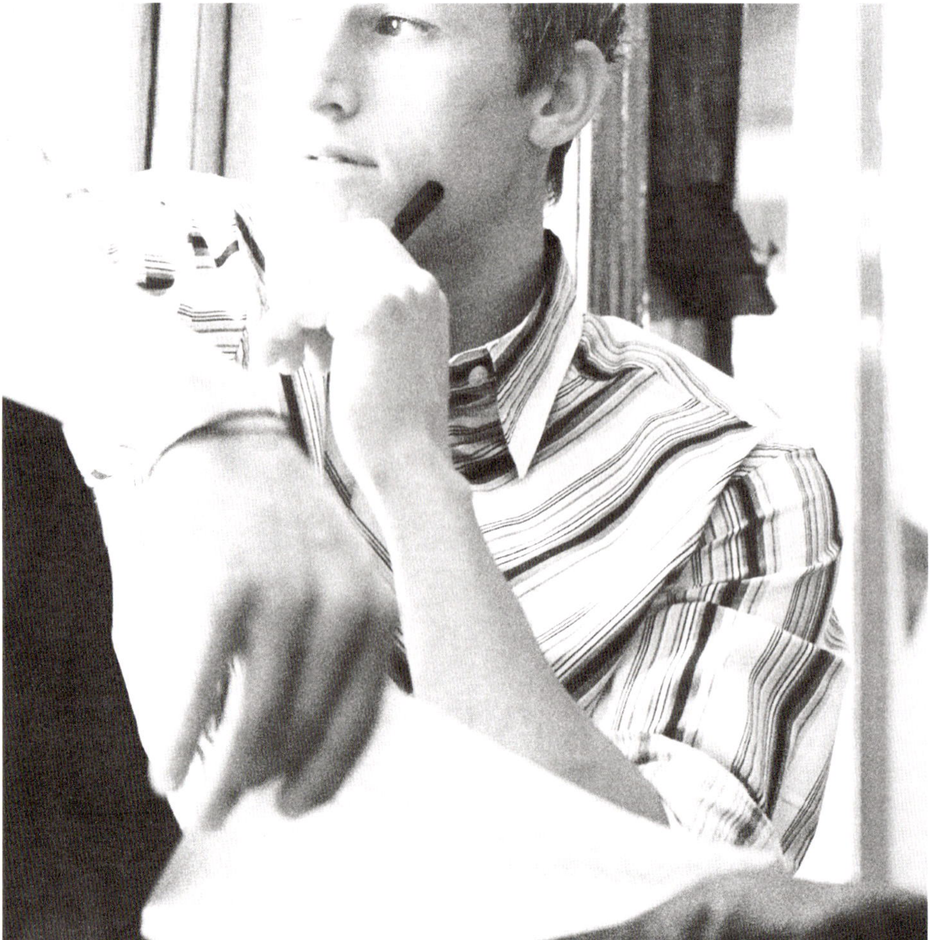

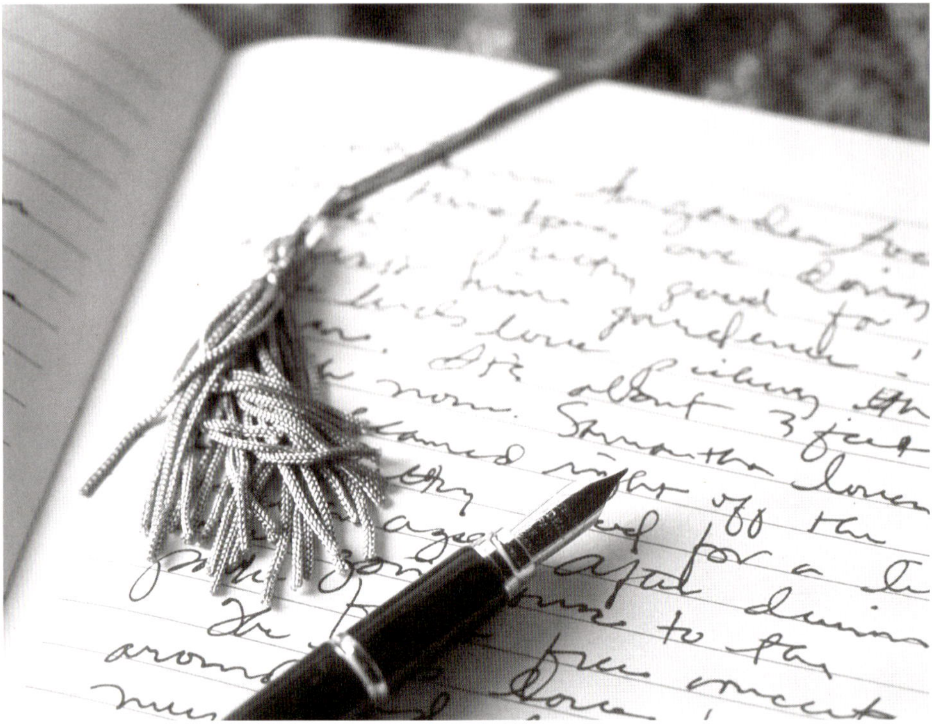

Here are a few messages of praise

Way to go! I am proud of you! - Aunt Denise

You have been simply the best Geth. - Steph ♡

Congratulations Big D!!! ♡ little B

REMEMBER! HIS OLD MEN-! YOU'LL BE FINE! Mr. Them

ENJOY COLLEGE, BUT NOT TOO MUCH. Tom & Monta

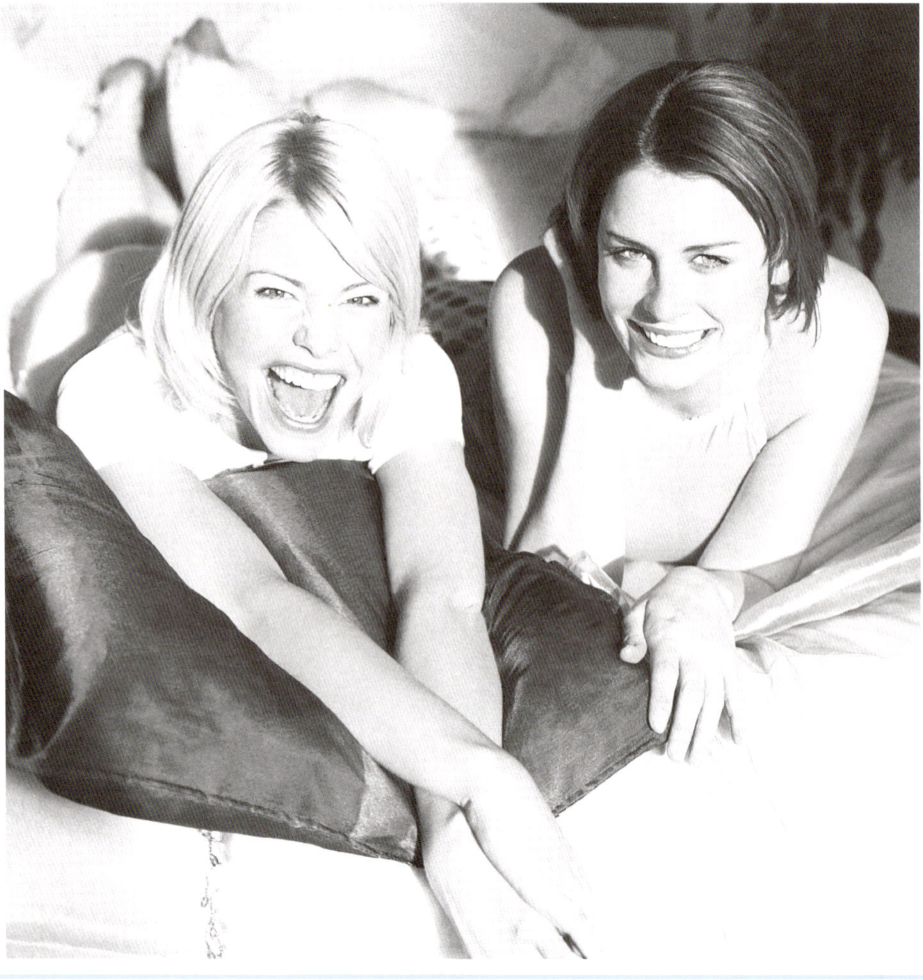

The best things in life are right now!

A toast to the treasured

I know you'll always remember

OBX, O.C., weeks at the mountain house during lazy summer months, Apple Butter Festivals, mountain house Christmas and just spending time together. Dutch Wonderland, Double Rock Park, N.Y at eighteen, Disney Ice Shows, Easter egg hunts, annual Christmas shopping and so much more.

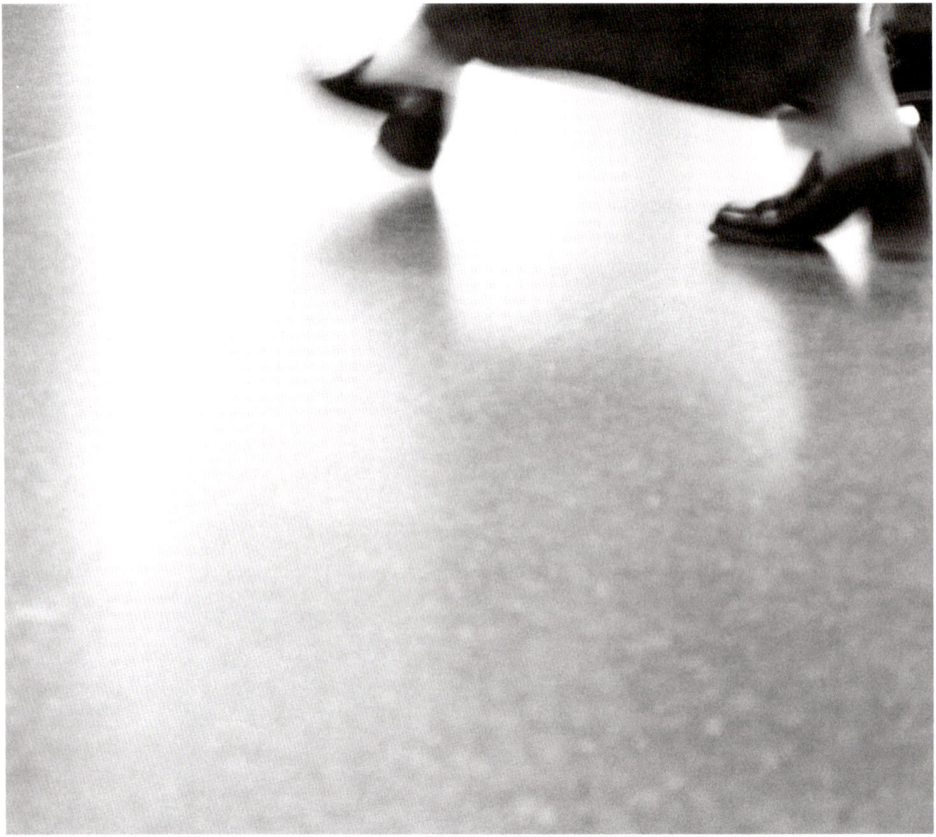

Your future begins with today!

Congratulations

I remember the night

There were times you felt

Remember this

Senior year, you had four AP tests over eight days - AP Psychology, AP Calculus BC, AP Biology, and AP English Literature. Somehow, through a small miracle, you studied, completed and passed w/ nothing less than a 4) on every single one!

I have only praise for

all the homework you did.

The project that became a part of you was

the YEARBOOK.

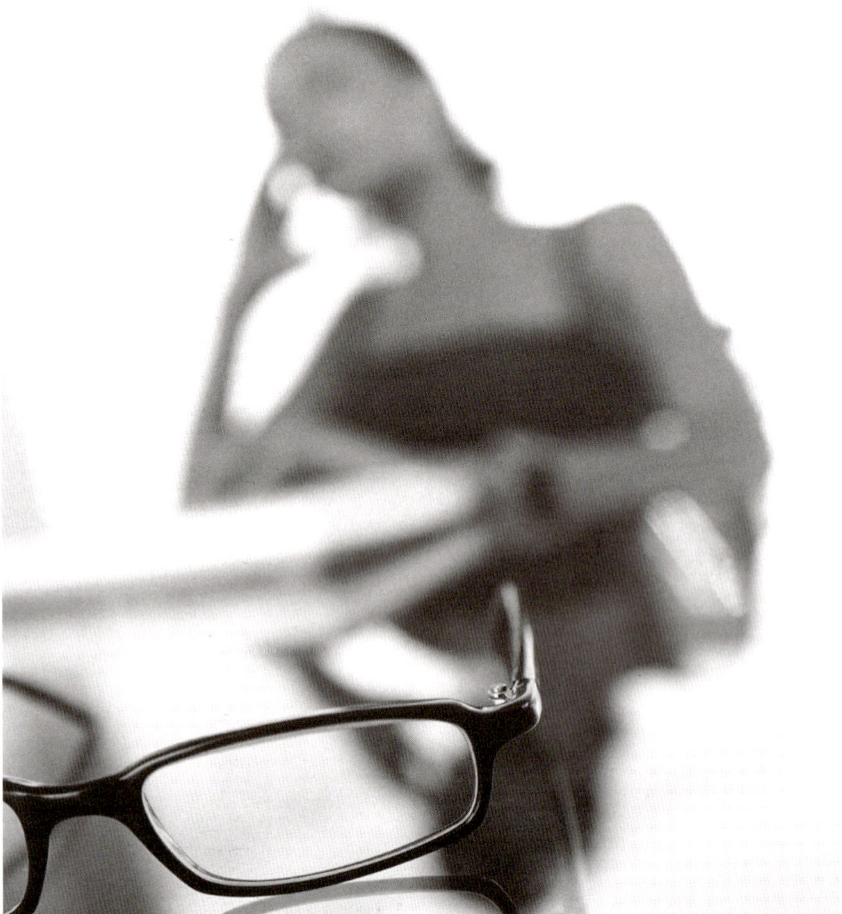

*There is a
simple way
to look at life...
every day is
an opportunity.*

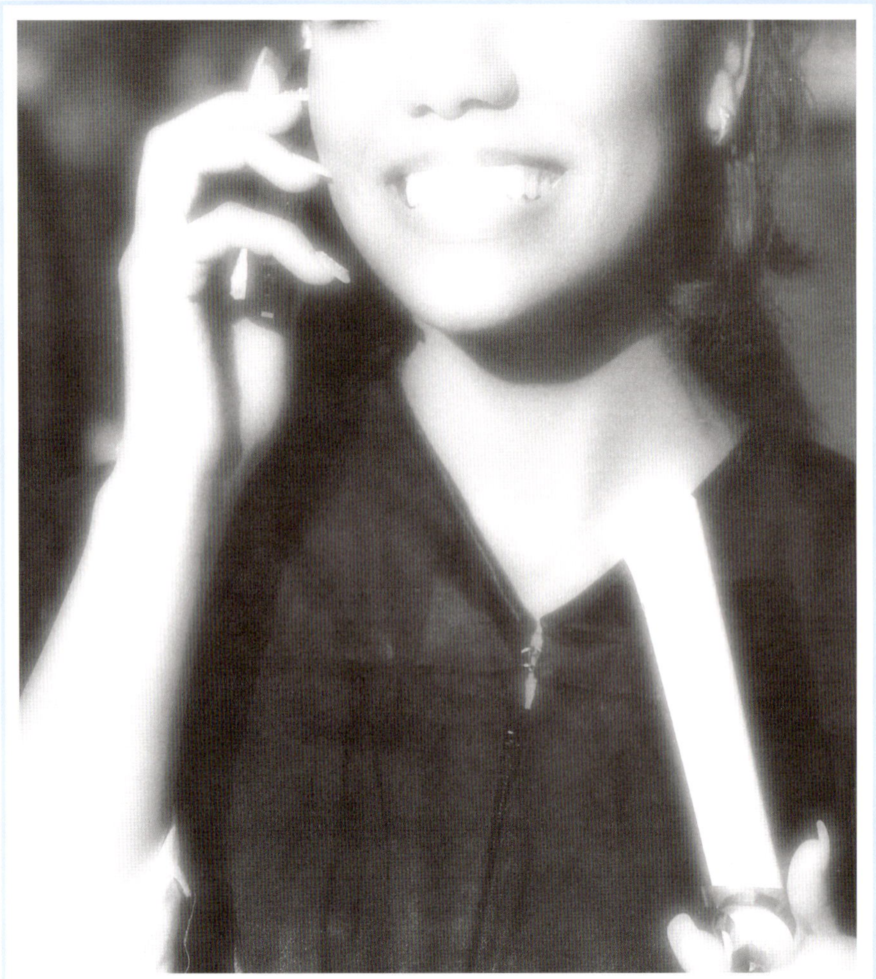

Remember all the tomorrows you dreamed about? They are today!

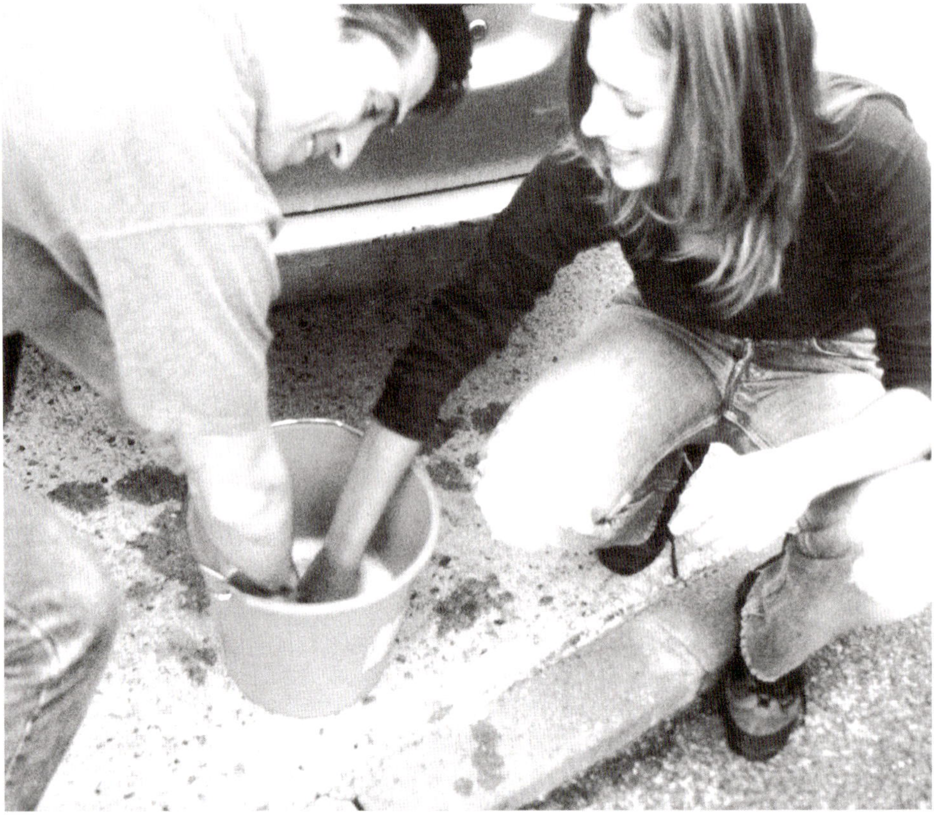

Friends that have enriched your life

Maddie Swift.

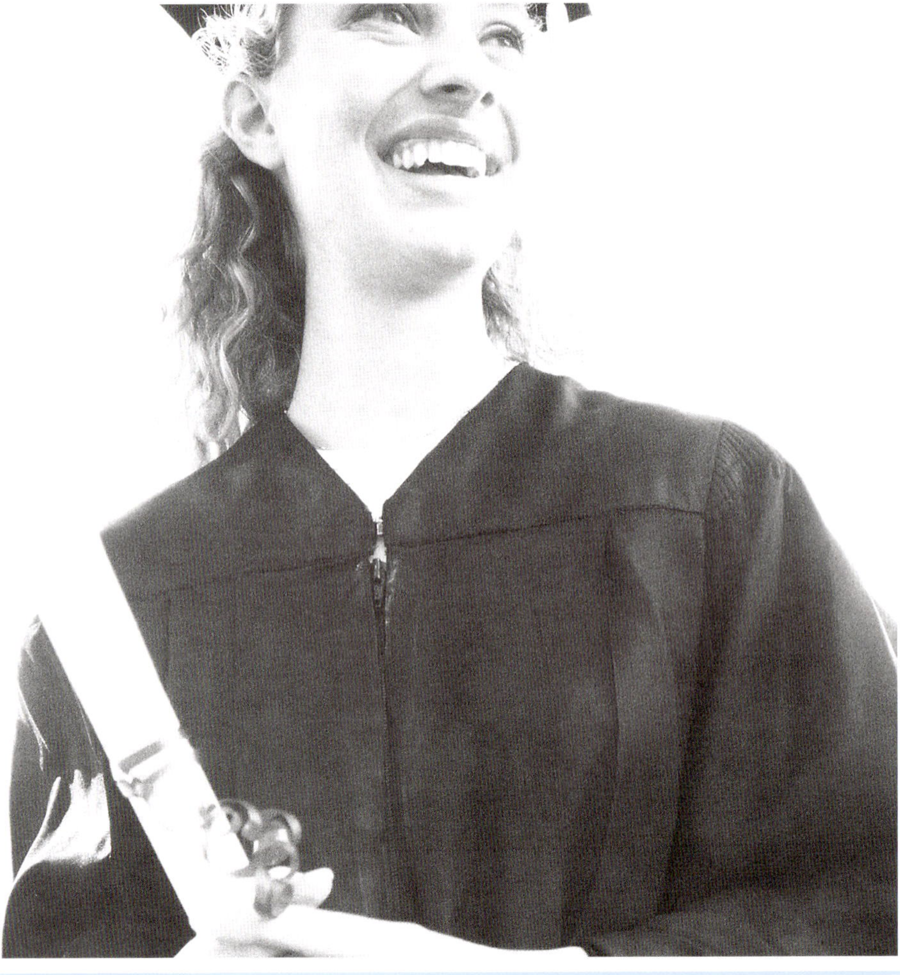

*You
have arrived!*

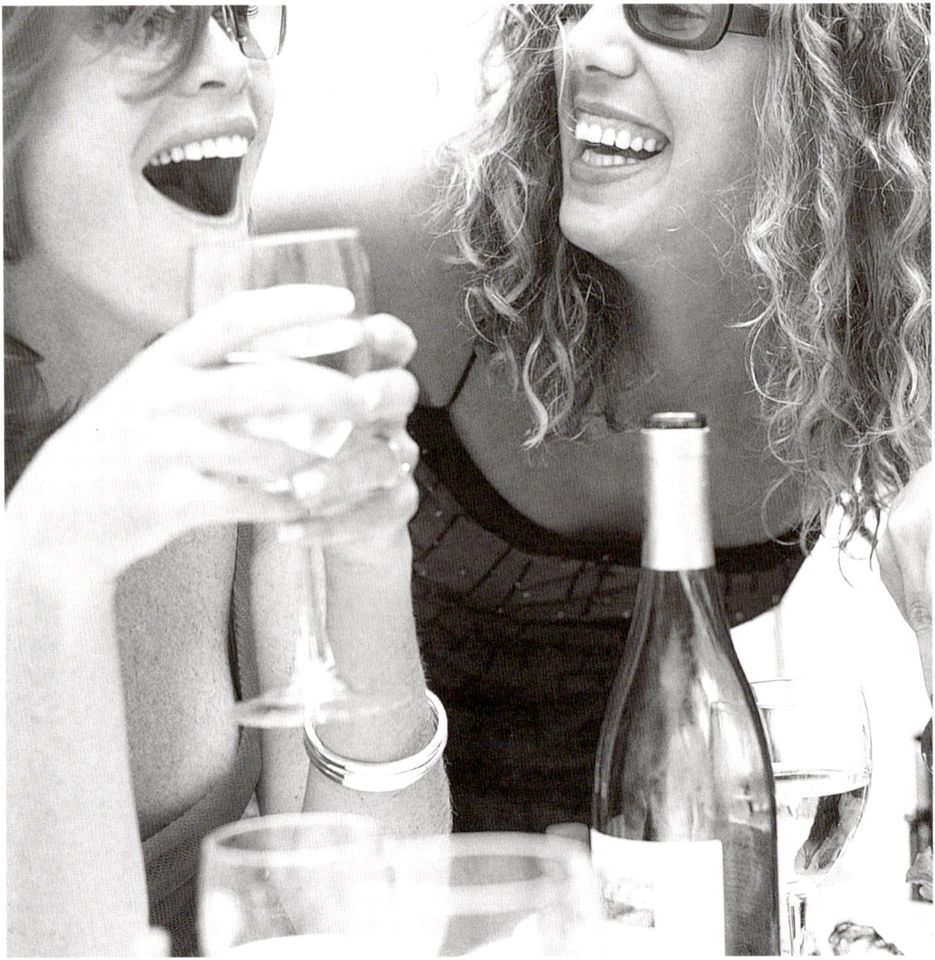

*May there be
the best days of your life!*

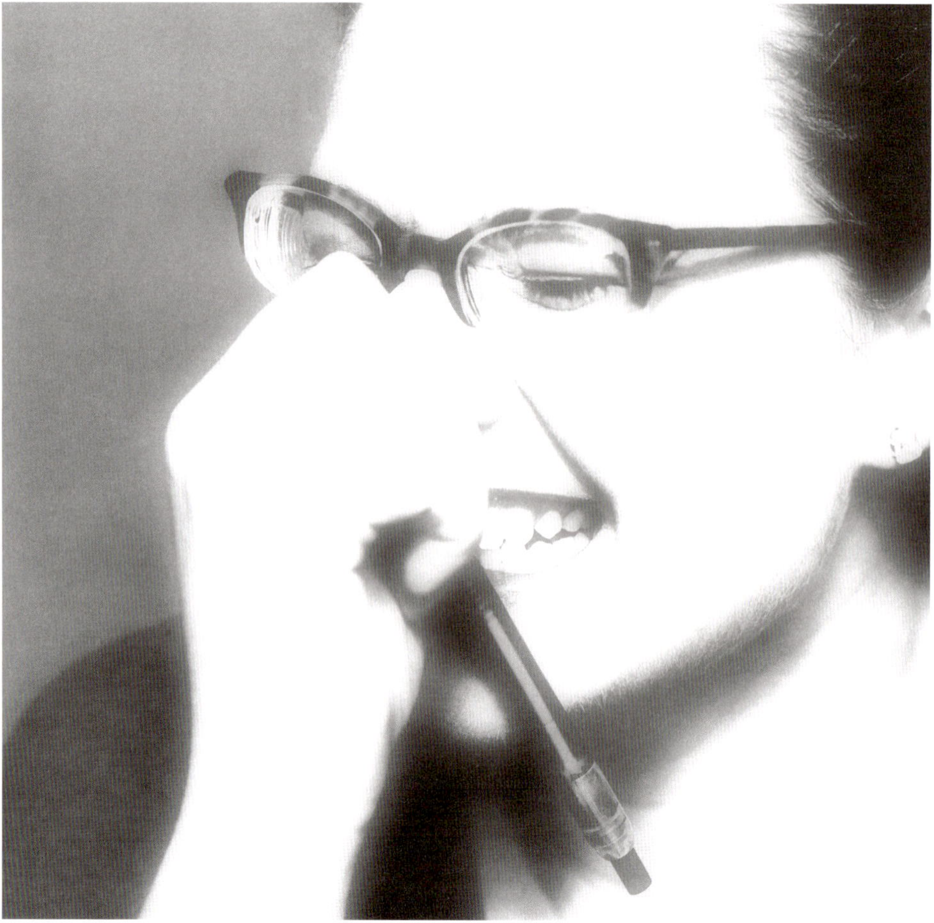

Your hard work reaps rewards.

Congratulations!
With experience like

...this behind you...

You are bound for the good life of

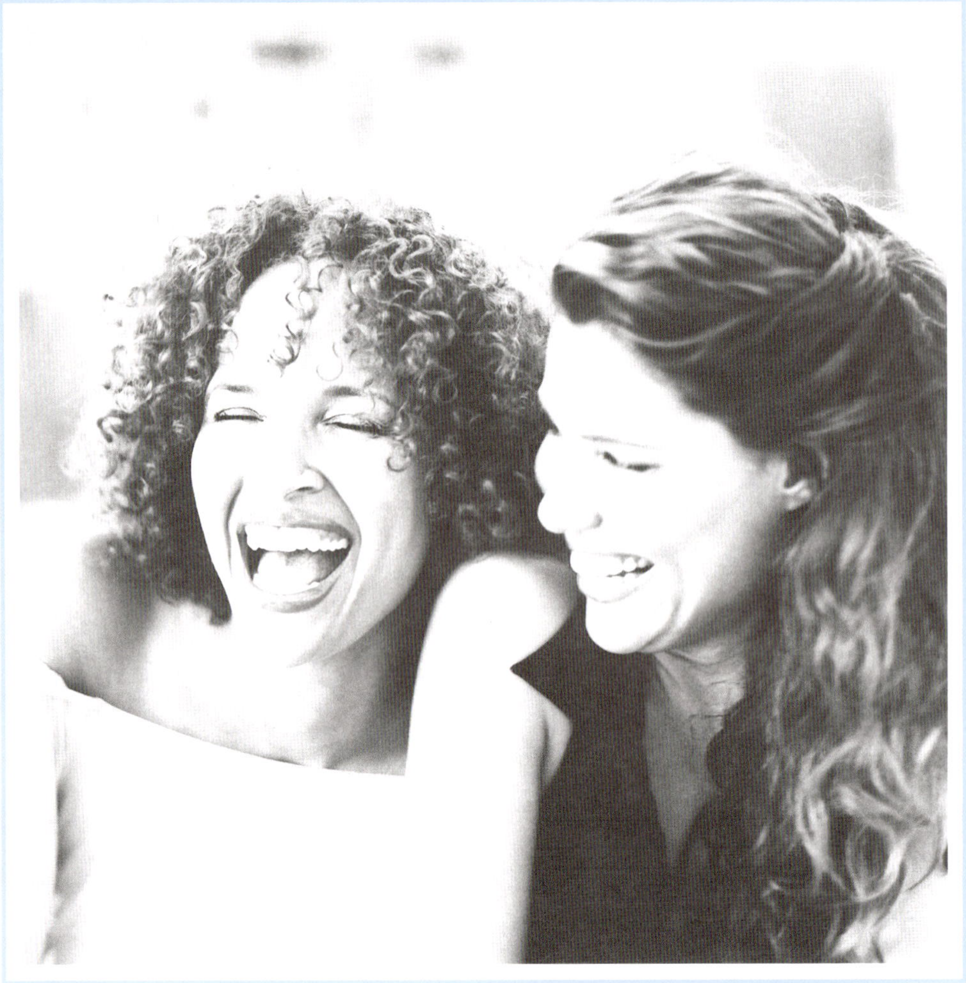

No matter where
your life takes you,
I'll always
be there for you.

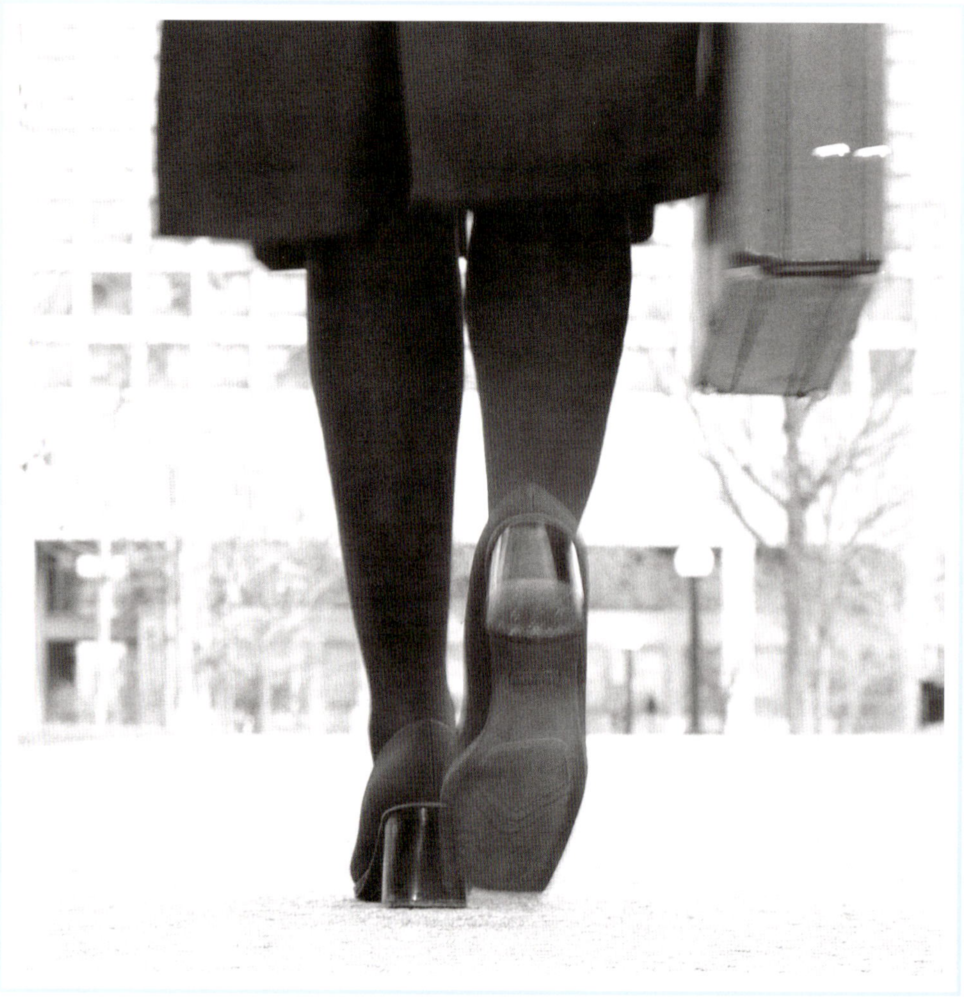

Life has a way of appreciating of your efforts... success!

© 2004 Havoc Publishing
San Diego, California
U.S.A.

Text by Maureen Webster

ISBN 0-7416-1314-X

All rights reserved.
No part of this publication may be reproduced or
transmitted in any form or by any means, electronic or
mechanical, including photocopying, recording, any
information storage and retrieval system without
permission in writing from the publisher.

www.havocpub.com

Made in Korea